G. SCHIRMER'S
COLLECTION OF
OPERA LIBRETTOS

DIE FLEDERMAUS

Operetta in Three Acts

Music by

Johann Strauss

English Adaptation
by
RUTH and THOMAS MARTIN

Ed. 2558

G. SCHIRMER, *Inc.*

DISTRIBUTED BY
HAL•LEONARD®
CORPORATION
7777 W. BLUEMOUND RD. P.O. BOX 13819 MILWAUKEE, WI 53213

45605c

DIE FLEDERMAUS

Maximilian Steiner, director of the Theater an der Wien in Vienna had bought the rights to a French play called *Le Réveillon*. After having studied it more closely, he found it unsuitable for the Viennese public and tried to discard it. Not being able to do so, he commissioned two writers, Richard Genée and Karl Haffner, to adapt the play. So *Le Réveillon* was transformed into *Die Fledermaus* (The Bat).

Johann Strauss, to whom the composition of the music was entrusted, was enthralled and secluded himself in his villa in Hietzing to work on it. After a few weeks, he emerged with the completed score.

Strangely enough, the first performance, in Vienna, 1874 (April 5 to be exact), received a cool reception. The Berlin production which followed was, however, a rousing success, and a revival in Vienna during the following season, equally well received, established *Die Fledermaus* once and for all.

Die Fledermaus is Strauss's third operetta, the two preceding ones being *Indigo* (1871) and *Karneval in Rom* (1873), both produced at the Theater an der Wien.

The first performance in the United States was given in German at the Thalia Theater in New York in 1879, and the first performance in English at the Casino Theater in New York.

THE STORY

ACT I. Gabriel von Eisenstein has been sentenced to eight days in prison for a minor offense. He is about to leave for jail when Falke, his friend, persuades him to postpone surrendering and go instead to a ball that Prince Orlofsky is giving. Falke has a little scheme in revenge for a practical joke Eisenstein once played upon him: (After a very gay masquerade, Eisenstein had abandoned the sleeping and intoxicated Falke, costumed as a bat, in a public park, where he awakened to the jeers of the promenaders on a Sunday morning.) Elaborating his plan, Falke also invites Rosalinda, Gabriel's wife, Adele, her maid, and Frank, the prison warden, to the ball, where all are to appear under assumed identities.

After a touching farewell Eisenstein departs, and Alfred, a former admirer of Rosalinda's, appears and finding her alone, makes love to her while singing and drinking her husband's champagne. Soon, however, Warden Frank appears in order to escort Eisenstein to jail, or, as he jokingly puts it, his "Lovely, lively pigeon-house." Alfred, in order to spare Rosalinda and himself the embarrassment of explaining the compromising circumstances, allows Frank to believe he is Eisenstein and goes to jail.

ACT II. The party at Orlofsky's is in progress. The Prince, very rich and very bored, is the host. Adele appears, wearing one of her mistress's ball-gowns. Eisenstein, posing as Marquis Renard, recognizes her, but Adele brazens out the situation to the bitter end, insisting that she is a successful actress. Rosalinda arrives, masked, and is introduced as an Hungarian countess who will remain masked because she has a very jealous husband. Eisenstein makes love to his own wife, and she succeeds in taking his repeater-watch away from him—a souvenir to be used as evidence of his misbehavior. The party breaks up at dawn.

ACT III. Alfred has spent the night in a cell, supervised by Frosch, the merry drunken jailer. Frank, still tipsy, arrives to take over. Adele, who wants to be a real actress, comes to beg Frank, or the Chevalier Chagrin as she knows him, to further her career. Eisenstein finally reports for jail, Rosalinda arrives, and eventually everyone's true identity is revealed. Falke confesses that the evening was all his plotting and a good joke on everyone, aided by the culprit, Champagne.

CAST OF CHARACTERS

GABRIEL VON EISENSTEIN, a banker . . . . Tenor

ROSALINDA, his wife . . . . Soprano

ALFRED, a singer . . . . Tenor

ADELE, chambermaid to the Eisensteins . . . . Coloratura Soprano

BLIND, a lawyer . . . . Tenor buffo

Dr. FALKE, friend of Eisenstein . . . . Baritone

FRANK, prison warden . . . . Baritone

SALLY, Adele's sister . . . . Soprano

FROSCH, jailer (speaking role) . . . . Comedian

PRINCE ORLOFSKY, young, rich, elegant* . . . . Singing Actor

IVAN, major-domo of Orlofsky . . . . Actor

Guests at Orlofsky's party; Waiters and the Ballet.

* The part of Orlofsky should be sung by a man.

TIME: about 1850

PLACE: near Vienna

SYNOPSIS OF SCENES

DIE FLEDERMAUS

ACT I

Room in a summer villa of Eisenstein, near Vienna.

At rear R. a doorway, leading to an anteroom and the outside. S.L. a practicable window. Front L. a door, leading to the adjoining room. Front L. a settee, at rear a dresser with mirror. At R. a table with chairs. Near door a bell-pull.

It is late afternoon.

No. 1. INTRODUCTION

ALFRED (*offstage*)

Turtle dove who flew aloft,
Calm my pain enraptured.
Turtle dove I kissed so oft,
Let thyself be captured!
Dearest, sweetest turtle dove,
Come, let nothing hinder;
Full of ardor is my love,
Darling Rosalinda!

(*Toward the end of the song, Alfred climbs through the window into the room. Noticing that it is empty, he says:*)

Wasting this glorious voice of mine on an empty room!

(*exits through window*)

ADELE

(*entering with open letter in her hand*)
This is from my sister Sally
Who's a member of the ballet:
"We are going to a party
Which I promise will be gay.
Prince Orlofsky, the talk of the town,
Will be the host at this superb affair.
If you're clever, you can borrow
One of your lady's fancy dresses.
She has so many, she won't miss one,
And you can't miss a chance like this one.
Get the night off, tell a story,
Then show up in all your glory.
You will see there's nothing better!"
Says my little sister's letter.

Much as I would love to go,
It's not as easy as it sounds.
If my lady should say no,
What would I do?
I wish I knew, I wish I knew! Ah!
Could I be that turtle dove
I would soar to clouds above!
I could fly to far-off borders,
Not a soul to give me orders!
Why, oh, why did destiny
Make a chambermaid of me?

ALFRED (*sings*)

Turtle dove who flew aloft,
Calm my pain enraptured,

ADELE (*speaks, during music*)

A street singer? My, he sounds awfully good!

ALFRED (*sings*)

Turtle dove I kissed so oft,
Let thyself be captured . . .

ADELE (*speaks*)

He must be an opera singer. I'll have to give him something.

(*starts for the window*)

ALFRED

Dearest, sweetest turtle dove,
Come let nothing hinder.
Full of ardor is my love,
Darling Rosalinda . . .
Full of ardor is my love . . .

ADELE (*speaks*)

Darling who?

ALFRED (*sings*)

Darling Rosalinda.

ADELE

Darling Rosalinda? Why, he's not serenading me, he's serenading my mistress. I'll have to tell her.

(*calls out*)

My la—dy!

ROSALINDA

(*offstage, echoing Adele's tone*)

What is it?

ADELE

(*very slyly and meaningfully*)

There's someone asking for you!

1

ROSALINDA
(*entering, very gaily*)
Who is it? Where is he?

ADELE
(*pointing to the window*)
Down there!

ALFRED
(*offstage, below window, sings opening
bars of the Count's aria Ecco ridente
from* The Barber of Seville)
"Ecco ridente in cielo
Spunta la bella aurora"

ROSALINDA (*joyfully*)
It's he! It's Alfred!
(*changing to a matter-of-fact tone*)
No. It couldn't be!
(*Alfred, offstage, vocalizes scales up and
down.*)

ROSALINDA (*listening*)
It *is* he!
(*nostalgically*)
What love duets we used to sing together, and how romantic he was!

ADELE (*interested*)
Oh?

ROSALINDA (*changing tone, dryly*)
When we were studying at the conserv-
atory.
(*again reminiscing*)
I recognized him right away by his
tenor and his bravado. Only a tenor
could have such a bravado, and only
a man with bravado could have such
a tenor!

ADELE
Yes, my lady.

ROSALINDA (*with admiration*)
Imagine, right here in front of my husband's house, trying to compromise
me with his high "C"!
(*Alfred, offstage, vocalizes to high C
and cracks miserably.*)
Did I say high "C"?
(*Alfred vocalizes again, hits a beautiful
high C.*)

ROSALINDA (*swooning*)
He still loves me!
(*remains pensively near window*)

ADELE (*near door, whining*)
My poor old aunt!

ROSALINDA
(*in thought, without noticing Adele*)
I thought he was on tour in Italy.

ADELE
My poor aunt is so ill!
(*She watches Rosalinda to see whether
her act registers.*)

ROSALINDA
(*in thought, as before*)
I wouldn't mind seeing him again.

ADELE
May I have the night off?

ROSALINDA
(*without noticing Adele, pursuing her
thought*)
Impossible, it can't be.

ADELE
But she is so ill and alone!

ROSALINDA (*as before*)
It's out of question!

ADELE (*insisting*)
Please, let me go!

ROSALINDA
(*suddenly noticing Adele, turning
sharply*)
What did you say?

ADELE
Please let me go and visit my poor, sick
old aunt tonight!

ROSALINDA
(*knowing what Adele is up to, resigns*)
What's the matter with her this time?

ADELE
She has the measles.

ROSALINDA (*determined*)
Of course you *cannot* go. You may
catch them.

ADELE
But they are such measly measles!

ROSALINDA
Absolutely not. Have you forgotten that
my husband has to begin his five-day
prison term this evening?
(*to herself, getting an idea*)
This evening!
(*to Adele*)
It's been postponed three times already
and tonight he simply *has* to go.

ADELE

But I still don't know why they are locking him up.

ROSALINDA

Because the other night at a restaurant he hung a man's hat on the rack.

ADELE

Is that so bad?

ROSALINDA

Well, the man's head was still in it.
(*A bell rings. Adele exits to open.*)
Good heavens, it's Alfred!
(*with feigned indignation*)
The conceit of the man!
(*running to the dresser*)
How dare he disgrace me like this!
(*spraying herself with perfume, etc.*)
I won't let him in, if it's the last thing I do!
(*poses with the back to the window, facing the door S.R. in a theatrically exaggerated waiting pose*)
(*sweetly*)
Come in!

ALFRED

(*climbs through window, unnoticed by Rosalinda*)
Don't move! I want to remember you just as you are!
(*Rosalinda turns.*)
Oh, you moved!

ROSALINDA (*reproachfully*)

Did you have to come through the window?

ALFRED

(*with pathos, always theatrically, the typical opera tenor*)
And why not? Romeo—Juliet—the balcony!

ROSALINDA

(*not returning Alfred's enthusiasm*)
Alfred!

ALFRED

"Alfred" is it? Why not "*Caro Alfredo*," and fly to me with open arms?

ROSALINDA (*sternly*)

Sir, I am married!

ALFRED

But dearest, that does not disturb me at all!

ROSALINDA

But it does me. You must go.

ALFRED (*brazenly*)

I did not come here, just to—go.

ROSALINDA

If my husband should come home!

ALFRED

He won't. Everyone in town knows that he has to go to jail tonight.

ROSALINDA (*scared*)

Tonight! I beg you, I implore you! Leave me!

ALFRED (*gallantly*)

Very well. I'll leave, but on one condition: That I may return when your husband is in jail.

ROSALINDA

No!

ALFRED

(*more and more theatrically*)
Swear to me that you'll receive me! Giurami, Carissimaaa!
(*falls into singing loudly*)

ROSALINDA

(*putting her hand on his mouth, cutting his tone off*)
Anything, anything to make you leave! I swear!

ALFRED

Well then, I'll go.
(*starts toward door*)

ROSALINDA (*as if hurt*)

Where are you going?

ALFRED (*returning quickly*)

You told me to go!

ROSALINDA (*sweetly*)

Goodbye!

ALFRED (*with pathos*)

Not "goodbye," but: "until we meet again." Tonight, at eight.

ROSALINDA

Goodbye!
(*Noise of loud voices is heard outside.*)

ALFRED

Good Lord!
(*runs back frantically*)

ROSALINDA

Good heavens, my husband!

ALFRED

Your husband? But I don't like husbands!

ROSALINDA

You must hide!

(*pushes Alfred toward room S.L.*)

ALFRED

Where?

ROSALINDA

In there!

(*She pushes Alfred into the other
room.*)

ALFRED (*sticking out his head*)

In here?

ROSALINDA

Alfred!!

(*pushes him back into the other room*)

(*Eisenstein enters, arguing loudly with
Blind, his lawyer.*)

No. 2 Terzet

EISENSTEIN

(*speaks while introduction is played*)

Of all the lawyers in Vienna, I had to
choose you!

(*sings*)

When these lawyers don't deliver,
They will sell you down the river,
My attorney is a clown!

ROSALINDA

Quiet down!

BLIND

Quiet down!

EISENSTEIN

All he did when he defended
Was to get my term extended,
And it's he who let me down!

BLIND

Let you down?

ROSALINDA

Let you down, he let you down?

EISENSTEIN

Yes! He's the biggest fool in town.

ROSALINDA

What did he do?

BLIND

It's n . . not true!

EISENSTEIN

You soon will see!

ROSALINDA

What shall I see? Explain to me.

EISENSTEIN

Listen to me.

BLIND

No, first li-listen to me!

EISENSTEIN

How dare you say another word?
For such a thing there's no explaining!

BLIND

I be-believe you are complaining?

ROSALINDA

Don't make a scene, what do you
mean?

EISENSTEIN

My lawyer got me in the soup!

BLIND

You treat me like a nincompoop!

EISENSTEIN

You're only talking tommyrot!

BLIND

Your te-te-temper is too hot!

EISENSTEIN

You drive me ma-ma-mad!

BLIND

You lo-lo-lose your head.

EISENSTEIN

You are a charlatan!

BLIND

You are no gentleman!

EISENSTEIN, BLIND

You are the only one to blame,
You have a feeble scatterbrain!

ROSALINDA

Why waste your precious voice,
You have no other choice!

(*to Blind*)

I would suggest you disappear,
Or there will be a scandal here!

EISENSTEIN

I would suggest you disappear,
Or there will be a scandal here.
Yes, go away!
Get out of here!

BLIND

It's be-be-best to disappear!
I'll go away, away from here!
I'll disappear!
(*Exit.*)

ROSALINDA

Be calm, my sweet, I beg of you;
The court has spoken; that is true.
Within five days, if you surrender,
If you surrender you can set the matter
straight.

EISENSTEIN

Five days, do you say? Now it is eight!
They made my sentence three days
longer!
This awful mess is all his fault!
This very day I must appear.
If I don't go, they will come here.

ROSALINDA

That goes too far, I must admit it.

EISENSTEIN

You see!

ROSALINDA

Ah, my darling Gabriel!
Confined inside a lonely cell,
What can I say that will console you?
What shall I do without you?

EISENSTEIN

When these lawyers make a blunder,
One is sold right out from under.
It's enough to drive me mad!

ROSALINDA

It is really very bad!

BLIND (*reappearing*)

Who is bad?

ROSALINDA

You are bad!

EISENSTEIN

It's enough to drive me mad!

BLIND

When your prison term is through,
We shall go to court and sue.
Then I'll sho-sho-show you
All the tricks that I can do:
I'm emphatic, problematic, a fanatic,
I'm asthmatic,
I'm magnetic, anaesthetic, alphabetic,
apathetic,
I'm pugnacious, disputatious, I'm lo-
quacious, I'm fallacious,
I'm objective, recollective, introspec-
tive, ineffective,

I'm prolific, scientific. In a word, I am
te-terrific.
Su-su-sure I'll win the case.

ROSALINDA

That's enough, that's enough, it is
enough!

ROSALINDA, EISENSTEIN

You may plead and argue all day long,
No matter what you do, you're wrong,
You'll never win a single case,
Ah no, you'll never win a case.
You'll never win a litigation.

ROSALINDA

Ah, the way these lawyers blunder,
All is lost, it is no wonder!
You could really lose your calm!

EISENSTEIN

When these lawyers make a blunder
You are sold right out from under,
You could really lose your calm!

ROSALINDA, EISENSTEIN

All he did when he defended
Was to get his (my) term extended.
He alone has done the harm!

BLIND

Why do clients, now I wonder,
Always bellow, rage, and thunder?
You could really lose your calm!
All he did, when he offended,
Was to get his term extended,
He alone has done the harm!
(*During Terzet, Alfred steals away and
exits through window, while Eisen-
stein pushes Blind out through the
door.*)

ROSALINDA

(*alone with Eisenstein*)

Then your sentence has been increased?
To eight days?

EISENSTEIN

For this bonus, this lovely bonus, I have
to thank Mr. Blind!

BLIND (*re-entering*)

Don't thank m-me! You d-did it all by
yourself, s-single-handed. You completely infu-furiated the j-j-his honor.
But d-don't w-wo-fret. If they s-send
you to j-j-prison again, I'll d-defend
you again. No hard feelings.

EISENSTEIN (*furiously*)

Yes, I shall most certainly call on you.
(*while throwing him out*)
Now get out of here, and don't let me
lay eyes on you again.
(*coming back from the door*)
There ought to be a law against such
lawyers!

BLIND (*returning*)

I'll send you the b-bill the first of the
month.

(*Eisenstein throws him out again.*)

ROSALINDA (*babying Eisenstein*)

My poor darling Gabriel. Eight days!
And you really have to go tonight?
(*helps him out of his jacket*)

EISENSTEIN (*dejected*)

Tonight.

ROSALINDA

(*helping him into his house robe*)
How could they sentence a man with
your personality! They are barbari-
ans!

EISENSTEIN

I wouldn't mind their locking up my
personality, but they insisted that I
go along too. I finally coaxed them
into letting me come home for my
last meal with you.

(*rings bell-pull*)

ADELE (*enters, tearfully*)

You rang, sir?

EISENSTEIN

What are you crying about?

ADELE

My poor old aunt!
(*cries*)

ROSALINDA

Her poor old aunt is ill again!

ADELE

She is dying now!

EISENSTEIN

I thought she died last week!

ADELE (*forgetting herself*)

Oh, that was my grandmother.

ROSALINDA (*getting impatient*)

Enough, Adele, you can't go.

EISENSTEIN

I'd like you to order us a very good
dinner.

ADELE

What would you like, sir?

EISENSTEIN

Use your imagination. A prisoner's last
meal—and hurry!

ADELE

A prisoner's last meal. Yes, sir.

(*exits S.R.*)

EISENSTEIN

That reminds me, I'd better find something to wear, something appropriate
for jail.

ROSALINDA (*surprised*)

Appropriate for jail?

EISENSTEIN

I mean, something that won't look out
of place among thieves and cut-
throats. After all, it's my first contact
with the underworld, and I have to
make a success of it.

(*goes into room S.L.*)

ADELE

(*enters, crying hard, announcing*)
Boo-hooooo! Dr. Falke. Boo-hooooo!

FALKE (*enters, gaily*)

My compliments, loveliest of all ladies.

(*noticing Adele*)
What's the matter with you?

ADELE

My grandmother died again!

(*holds hand to mouth, exits quickly*)

FALKE

With all my heart I congratulate you
on getting rid of your tyrant for eight
days. Is he still there?

(*Rosalinda motions to the other room*)

(*Falke, loudly, to Eisenstein, through
the door*)

And congratulations to you too, my
friend, for getting three days added
to your sentence. That really took
genius!

ROSALINDA

Don't tease him, doctor. Poor darling.
Try to cheer up our convict a little,
and I'll see that everything is in order
for tonight.
(*to herself, while on her way to door
S.R., very gaily, almost singing*)
Tonight, tonight, tonight!

EISENSTEIN

(*entering from S.L., dejected*)
Hello, Falke.

FALKE (*very gaily*)

Gabriel, my boy, I am going to cheer
you up.

EISENSTEIN

(*sitting down on settee*)
Impossible. I was never so depressed in
my life.

FALKE

Wait, until you hear. I came to invite
you to a magnificent party tonight.

EISENSTEIN

Are you mad? I have to go to jail in an
hour.

FALKE

You can go there tomorrow morning.
But tonight, you're coming with me
to a party at the villa of Prince
Orlofsky.

EISENSTEIN

Orlofsky? That mad Russian? The one
everyone is talking about this season?
The one whose guests take bubble
baths in champagne?

FALKE

That's exactly whom I mean, and tonight's guest list is the best ever. I'm
arranging the Prince's social life since
he's new in town.

EISENSTEIN

You tempt me. But I really don't dare.

FALKE

Don't be silly. No one will ever find out.
Besides, the Prince begged me to ask
only the most intelligent, brilliant
people. So you *have* to come. You
can't disappoint me.

EISENSTEIN (*flattered*)

Well, that's true. I have a reputation of
being—let's say—the life of the party.

FALKE

And you do have delightfully eccentric
ideas for practical jokes.

EISENSTEIN

The elephant never forgets—or shall I
say, the "Bat"? Ha, ha, ha!

FALKE (*humoring him*)

Ha, ha, ha! Oh, yes, Mr. "Butterfly."
You certainly made a fool of me that
time.

EISENSTEIN (*remembering*)

Just about three years ago.

FALKE

At our fraternity's masquerade ball in
Grinzing!

EISENSTEIN

I was a Butterfly!

FALKE

And I was a Bat!

EISENSTEIN

And you went on a bat to end all bats!
Were you drunk!

FALKE

And you drove me "home"—

EISENSTEIN (*highly amused*)

Only you never got there . . . because—

FALKE

You dumped me on a park bench . . .

EISENSTEIN

And when you woke up in broad day-
light, you were surrounded by all the
Sunday promenaders . . .

FALKE

And had to walk all the way home,
dressed as a bat!

EISENSTEIN (*happily*)

I'll never forget it!

FALKE (*with significance*)

Nor will I, Gabby old boy!

EISENSTEIN

Hm?

FALKE (*in a joking tone*)

Nor will I.

EISENSTEIN (*weakening*)

You know, if I went to the ball tonight,
it would be just like old times.

FALKE

And you could even take your little repeater-watch along.

EISENSTEIN

Heavens, yes. My greatest asset.
(*He lets the watch chime a few times.*)
It's an infallible girl-catcher!

FALKE

You promise it to all of them—

EISENSTEIN

And give it to none. That's the secret of my success!

FALKE

Then I can count on you?

EISENSTEIN

Well—

No. 3. Duet

FALKE

Come along to the ball,
It will raise your morale!
Jail can wait, why should you worry?
There's no need for such a hurry,
You have time for one more spree,
Come and have some fun with me.
You will meet the whole ballet,
All the pretty ballerinas,
Mad'moiselles and signorinas,
They're so lovely and petite.
My dear fellow, what a treat,
What a treat!
With blondes and brunettes we will
  dance and dine,
And shower confetti and revel in wine.
In fun and flirtation the hours will fly.
It's one invitation you can't pass by.
Admit that a party like this can't fail
To put you in shape for your term in
  jail.
Do you agree?

EISENSTEIN

Yes, I agree.
But Rosalinda must never know.

FALKE

Kiss her good-night, and off we go!
Say: "Fare you well, my pretty kitten!"

EISENSTEIN

No, no, "my lambkin," I shall say,
"My sweetest lambkin!"

FALKE

"Sweetest lambkin."

EISENSTEIN

While she's sleeping peacefully
I will be the wolf!

FALKE

While she's sleeping peacefully
You will be the wolf,
And under the cover of dark,
Instead of to jail, you embark
With me on a heavenly lark!

EISENSTEIN

With you on a heavenly lark!

FALKE

I'll present you as a distinguished
  foreigner.
Your name will be Marquis Renard.
No one will be one bit the wiser.
Say yes!

EISENSTEIN

Well, I might be persuaded, but if—

FALKE

Now don't be a coward.
You owe it to yourself, old boy!

EISENSTEIN

You are right, you are absolutely right!

FALKE

You really will have a delightful time.

EISENSTEIN

Since I'm doing time for another crime,
I might as well add one more to the list.

FALKE

You might as well add one more to the
  list,
You'll come then?

EISENSTEIN

How can I resist?
Yes, I'll go with you!

FALKE

This chance is really too good to be
  true!

EISENSTEIN

To a supper fit for kings,
We shall go with hearts delighted,
Lovely women are invited,
Everybody laughs and sings.
Lalalalalalalalalalalalalala.
(*At the end of the Duet, Falke and
Eisenstein are dancing wildly, until
Eisenstein falls exhausted on the set-
tee, while Falke strikes a pose.*)

ROSALINDA

(*who has entered toward the end of the music and seen the men dancing*)

What on earth is going on here?

FALKE

(*collecting himself, a little embarrassed*)

I was just showing him some exercises to keep his blood in circulation while he is out of circulation.

EISENSTEIN

And he succeeded completely.

(*pretends to exercise a little more*)

FALKE

And now I must be on my way.

ROSALINDA

(*gives him his hat, glad to see him go*)

So soon, doctor?

FALKE

Oh yes, indeed, I want to leave you two dear people alone to make your fond farewells. I know how it is at a time like this.

(*to Eisenstein, softer*)

Don't forget, Marquis Renard is your name!

ROSALINDA

What did he say?

EISENSTEIN

He—just—wanted me to bring along my key when I came.

FALKE

(*quickly, to help out*)

Goodbye, lovely lady! Good luck—

(*while going*)

Mr. Butterfly!

EISENSTEIN

(*seeing Falke to the door*)

Goodbye, Mr. "Bat."

ROSALINDA (*sincerely*)

He's such a good friend!

EISENSTEIN

(*giggling, while leaving for room L.*)

He certainly is!

ROSALINDA (*alone*)

He's so happy, one would think he was going to a ball.

ADELE

(*enters, S.R., grumpily*)

May I have the supper served, my lady?

ROSALINDA

Yes, please. Mr. Eisenstein will be ready in a few minutes. By the way, Adele, I've been thinking things over, and I've decided to let you off tonight.

ADELE (*flabbergasted*)

You really mean it, my lady? Just before you absolutely refused.

ROSALINDA

I was a little upset then. Now I'm in the best of humor.

ADELE (*inquisitive*)

Because the master is being locked up?

ROSALINDA

That's enough, Adele. Be glad I let you go.

ADELE

Thank you, thank you very much, my lady.

ROSALINDA

Don't mention it. The pleasure is all mine.

(*calls to room S.L.*)

Darling! Supper is ready.

(*Eisenstein enters in full dress, very elegant, in great spirits, prances to the mirror to view himself.*)

What? Full dress for jail?

EISENSTEIN

Fine feathers make fine jailbirds!

ROSALINDA

Who said so?

EISENSTEIN

Falke. He said that the best people are going to jail these days. Doctors, lawyers, nobility—so you see—I'd better be on my way.

(*tries to skip away*)

ROSALINDA

But without your supper? Do you think it's wise on an empty stomach?

EISENSTEIN

Darling, I don't want to spoil my appetite for jail.

(*The music to No. 4 starts.*)

ROSALINDA

Aren't you even going to kiss me goodbye?

EISENSTEIN

Of course.

No. 4. Trio

ROSALINDA

To part is such sweet sorrow,
Such pain and such despair.
How shall I face tomorrow
Without my husband there?
With anguish and misgiving
I watch my love depart.
How can I go on living?
Oh Lord, it breaks my heart.
I dread this separation
Far more than I can say.
I'll live in desolation,
My husband gone away.
I'll think of you, dear, only,
When we are far apart,
And be so very lonely, ah!

EISENSTEIN (*sobbing*)

Oh Lord, it breaks my heart!

EISENSTEIN, ROSALINDA, ADELE

Oh Lord, it breaks my heart!
Oh goodness me, what misery!
How dreadful a calamity
Oh goodness me, what misery.
Oh goodness, gracious me!

ROSALINDA

Who'll waken me each morning
To ask me for his socks?
Who'll grumble for his paper,
Who'll wind the cuckoo clock?
And when the night is falling,
I'll get another shock.
My grief will be appalling.

ALL THREE

Oh goodness me, what misery, etc.

EISENSTEIN

What good is all this fretting?
There's nothing we can do.

ROSALINDA.

I find it most upsetting!

ADELE

And I feel badly, too!

EISENSTEIN

Farewell, I can't remain.

ROSALINDA, ADELE

Farewell, you can't remain,
Goodbye, goodbye, goodbye.

EISENSTEIN

Until we meet again.

ALL THREE

Until we meet again.
Oh Lord, it breaks my heart!
Oh goodness me, what misery, etc.

(*Eisenstein dances off. Adele follows.*)

ROSALINDA (*alone*)

Poor dear. It's awfully hard on him.
Our first separation since we're married.
(*sighing*)
How I wish I had time to grieve a little.
(*gaily*)
But I haven't, I haven't!
(*goes to the dresser*)

ADELE

(*entering from S.L. with a large
suitcase*)

Goodbye, my lady, I'm on my way.
(*tries to sneak out S.R.*)

ROSALINDA (*noticing the suitcase*)

Wait a minute! Why so much luggage?

ADELE

Oh, I'm taking a few extra things in
case of an emergency.

ROSALINDA

I see. Goodbye Adele.

ADELE

Goodbye, my lady.

ROSALINDA

And remember, don't go to close to
your poor sick aunt!

ADELE (*forgetting herself*)

Oh, I won't even go near her!
(*realizing her boner, exits quickly*)

ROSALINDA

Thank goodness, I'm rid of both of
them.

ADELE (*returning with a box*)

Package just arrived for you, my lady.

ROSALINDA

Put it on the chair.

(*Adele does so, snoops.*)
(*strongly*)

Goodbye, Adele.

(*Adele exits S.R.*)

Let's see—

(*opens the box*)

A mask, a wig, a note.

(*reads*)

"Dearest Rosalinda: If you want to see the man you married serving his term, wear this mask and wig, and come to Prince Orlofsky's palace tonight. There you will see him wining and dining with the dancing girls." The wretch!

(*continues reading*)

"You will be anounced as a Hungarian Countess. Do not fail me. Your devoted Falke."

(*furiously*)

Dancing girls! Dancing girls! And he's supposed to be in jail for eight measly days. When I get through with him, he'll be glad to go to jail for life!

ALFRED (*sings, offstage*)

Juuu—liet!

ROSALINDA (*forgetting herself, sings*)

Rooo—meo—oh, what am I going to do with that tempestuous tenor?

(*hurriedly takes up her greeting pose, this time in front of the window, with her back to the door*)

ALFRED (*enters through door S.R.*)

Juliet!

ROSALINDA (*turns, disappointed*)

Did you have to come through the door?

ALFRED

He's in jail, and we are alone.

ROSALINDA

And I am very unhappy.

ALFRED

Darling, I shall comfort you in French and Italian—

(*goes to table, starts to pour*)

Wine?

ROSALINDA

That you won't. I intend to remain uncomfortable.

ALFRED (*undaunted*)

Well, at least *I* intend to be comfortable.

(*pouring*)

Wine?

ROSALINDA (*pretending*)

I don't drink.

ALFRED

Well, I do.

(*pours himself wine*)

And now I shall assume the role of the legitimate master of the house. Let us imagine I am your husband.

ROSALINDA (*startled*)

My husband!

(*changing tone*)

That gives me an idea. *You are* going to take me to the ball.

ALFRED

(*busy with eating and drinking*)

Ball? What ball? Oh no. We are going to have a ball of our own right here.

ROSALINDA

No, we won't. You are coming with me. Go to my husband's wardrobe and dress for the occasion.

ALFRED

Dress for the occasion?

(*getting an idea*)

Alright, I'll do it.

(*Exit S.L., singing to himself.*)

ROSALINDA

(*furiously, going to the table*)

My faithful husband! My loving husband! Drinking champagne with dancing girls.

(*pours herself wine, and drinks. Then she notices Alfred, who has returned, dressed in Eisenstein's house-robe and cap with tassel.*)

(*Alfred throws himself upon the settee, relaxing luxuriously.*)

ROSALINDA (*petrified*)

Are you out of your mind?

ALFRED (*calmly, nonchalantly*)

Not at all. Now, about breakfast, tomorrow morning . . . let's see . . . we'll have coffee, rolls, Russian eggs . . .

ROSALINDA (*scandalized*)

Breakfast? Breakfast? Are you trying to compromise me?

ALFRED (*unconcerned*)

Yes—I mean—no. Darling, I'm not trying to compromise you. But neither do I intend to let the wine get warm.

(*gets up, goes to the table, pours wine for both*)

Let's drink and sing.

(*starts singing from* Traviata)

Libiamo, libiamo ne lieti calici . . .

ROSALINDA (*interrupting*)

No, no! No singing, please!

ALFRED

And why not? Once upon a time you loved to hear me sing.

(*Music No. 5 starts.*)

ROSALINDA (*weakening*)

That's just it. I loved not wisely, but too well.

No. 5. FINALE

ALFRED

Drink, my darling, drink to me!
Drink to all that used to be.
To the days we used to know
In the rosy long ago.
Love is but a fleeting dream,
Never born to last,
Like a sweet remembered theme
From the golden past.
When your youthful hopes depart,
Hopes that brought you happiness,
Wine will ease your troubled heart,
Bring forgetfulness.
Night and day,
Light and gay,
Let us sing our cares away.
Night and day,
Light and gay,
We sing our cares away.
Cling, cling, sing, sing,
Drink with me,
Sing with me,
Lalalalalala.

ROSALINDA

It's no use whatever,
He simply won't go.
He'll stay here forever.
No, no, no!

ALFRED

Drink on! Drink on! ah—
Drink my darling, drink to me,
Drink to all that used to be.
Do not frown so angrily,
Let me see you smile at me.
Once I was your dearest friend,
That is now a dream,
But tonight let us pretend
Dreams are what they seem.
Fancies bring us happiness
Though they soon may pass away.
Let's believe them nonetheless,
And enjoy today.

BOTH

Night and day, etc.

ROSALINDA (*speaks*)

I hear voices. Someone is talking! Heavens!

(*to Alfred*)

Listen! They are coming up the stairs!

ALFRED

Let them.

ROSALINDA

Heavens! What a situation!

FRANK

(*opens the door and speaks offstage*)
Wait for me outside.

(*enters*)

Do not be shocked, Madame. I am Prison Warden Frank and cannot resist the pleasure of coming personally to escort your recalcitrant husband into enforced seclusion.

ROSALINDA (*confused*)

But my husband is—

ALFRED

Drink, my darling, drink to me!
Drink to all that used to be!

ROSALINDA

Please be still, we are not alone.

ALFRED

Let us pretend we are. Cling, cling, etc.

FRANK

My carriage is waiting below, and I hope you will offer no further resistance.

ALFRED

No, no . . . Light and gay, etc.

FRANK

Ha, ha! Right you are. I see you take
the affair from the humorous side.

ALFRED

(*offering Frank a glass*)

Drink with me . . . etc.

FRANK

For all of me, ha ha ha!

BOTH

Night and day,
Light and gay,
Let us sing our cares away!

FRANK

A joke in its place is very fine.
Now do come with me, dear Mr. Eisenstein.

ROSALINDA (*to herself*)

What shall I do, where shall I go?

ALFRED

I am not your dear Eisenstein, I'm not
he, let me tell you . . .

FRANK

You are not he?

ALFRED

The devil, no!

FRANK

Come, come, be more civil!

ROSALINDA (*to Alfred*)

For heaven's sake say that you are!

FRANK (*to himself*)

I wonder what's behind all this?

ROSALINDA

Good sir, are you accusing me
Of any impropriety?
That would be quite absurd.
How can you think so ill of me
To question my integrity,
And doubt a lady's word?
Does the situation here
Not appear to be quite clear?
What man would dare
To stay right there
And have a tête-à-tête,
At half-past eight,
In such a state
Except my one and legal mate?

ALFRED, FRANK

What man would dare
To say right there, etc.

ROSALINDA

At night, when he's at home with me,
He always dines informally
In dressing gown and cap.
This intimate, domestic scene
Has always been his set routine.
See him yawn and nod his head.
How he longs to go to bed!
What man would wear
So free an air
In any lady's house!
So unimpressed,
And self-possessed,—
Except her one
And only spouse?

FRANK

No, no, you set my doubts at rest,
I'm sure you did not lie.
But come, dear Mr. Eisenstein,
And kiss your wife goodbye.

ROSALINDA

Kiss me goodbye?

ALFRED

Kiss her goodbye?

FRANK

Kiss her goodbye!

ROSALINDA

Well then, if you insist.
Now there you have this kiss!

ALFRED

Since I have nobly risen
To live your husband's life of crime,
Before I go to prison,
Come, kiss me just one more time!

FRANK

Enough, I must be on my way,
For I must go to a soirée.
Let's leave without delay,
So let us leave without delay!

(*goes toward the door, opens it, and
gives a sign to the policeman outside*)

ROSALINDA (*softly to Alfred*)

You surely will meet my husband as
well.

ALFRED

Perhaps we shall sleep in the very same
cell.

ROSALINDA

Be still, I implore!

ALFRED

You may be sure!

ROSALINDA

Be still, I implore, ah—

ALFRED

You may be sure!

FRANK

Down there at the gate,
My horse and carriage wait.
So come, we shall be late.
My lovely, lively pigeonhouse
Is nice as it can be.
The birds who flutter in and out
Get food and lodging free.
I have just one more vacancy,
A cozy little nest;
If you will kindly come with me,
It will be yours immediately.
Don't miss this opportunity
To be my honored guest.

ALFRED

If it must be
Then I shall go.

ROSALINDA

Do it for me!
Then be it so.

FRANK

Come on, let's go!

ALFRED

I'll go, but not before
I've kissed my wife once more.

ROSALINDA

Enough, my friend, now please behave!

ALFRED

Another kiss will make me brave.

ROSALINDA

No, no, enough, you must be going.

ALFRED

One last kiss and then I'll be fortified.

FRANK

Enough domestic bliss, my friend,
Or there will never be an end.
Enough, enough, my friend!

ALL THREE

My (his) lovely, lively pigeonhouse etc.

ROSALINDA

Yes, yes, follow him to be his honored
   guest.
Go with him for my sake.
Ah yes, you'll help me out of this un-
   pleasant situation,
Yes, my friend, you must do this for me.
Go, ah, go with him, it must be so.

ALFRED

I yield for now and follow him
To be his honored guest.
I shall go for your sake.
Why did he disturb this pleasant
   situation?
Did he have to come and call for me?
Ah, yes, why, why did he disturb this
   pleasant situation,
For now it must be so.

FRANK

I beg you kindly follow me right away.
Come because I did accept an invita-
   tion,
Come, I beg you, come at once with
   me.
It must be, it must be so. Ah, come!

(*Alfred is led away by Frank.*)

ACT TWO

*Hall in Prince Orlofsky's palace. The
rear is open and leads to a garden.
Exits R. and L. front and rear. A
party is in full swing. Elegantly
dressed guests are assembled, servants
pour and serve champagne.*

No. 6. ENTR'ACTE AND CHORUS

CHORUS

What a joy to be here
On this wonderful occasion!
So unique, so delightful,
It's the party of the year!
Nothing could be more intriguing
Than this most enchanting atmosphere.
Let us all be happy while we may.
We still are young and gay.
For today, let's be gay,
Let's all be gay.
We will dance, we will sing,
We will have a celebration.
With a song and with laughter
Let us make the rafters ring.

A SERVANT

Hors d'oeuvres!

A GUEST

Please bring some to me!

SECOND SERVANT

Cherry brandy!

A GUEST

One right here for me.

THIRD SERVANT
Turkish candy!

A GUEST
Here!

FOURTH SERVANT
Sachertorte!

A GUEST
Please!

A GUEST
I'll have a cup of tea!

A GUEST
And coffee here for me!

A SERVANT
At once, at once!

SEVERAL LADIES
Coffee here!

SEVERAL GENTLEMEN
Bring us beer!

CHORUS
The golden moments swiftly pass,
We must enjoy them while we may,
So laugh and sing and fill your glass,
For today, let us play the night away,
For all too soon the moments pass,
Let us sing, let us play,
Let us dance the night away.
Let's be gay!
(*At the end of the music the guests disperse.*)

ADELE (*entering S.L. rear*)
Sally! Here I am!

SALLY (*shocked*)
Oh, good heavens, Adele! What are *you* doing here?

ADELE
What do you mean, what am I doing here?

SALLY
I am amazed to see you here, in a place like this!

ADELE
And I'm amazed at your amazement! Didn't you say in your letter . . .

SALLY
What letter?

ADELE
The one I got this afternoon where you told me I simply had to get the night off, borrow one of my lady's dresses, and come here to a wonderful party.

SALLY
I wrote that? Somebody's playing a joke on you.

ADELE
A joke? I had our old aunt lying in a coma, until I finally managed to get the night off, to say nothing of the trouble I went to to "borrow" my lady's gown and sneak it out of the house. And now you don't even want to be seen with me!

SALLY
Well, after all! A chambermaid in such a gathering! You're not very *à propos*.

ADELE
Oh no?
(*pulls up her dress a bit, uncovering her leg*)
Take a look at that.

SALLY (*shocked*)
Adele!

ADELE
That's *à propos* enough.

SALLY
Stop it, for goodness sake!

ADELE
I will, as soon as you stop acting so conceited. After all you're not a dancer because you can dance so well. I know how you arrived. And dancing had very little to do with it.

SALLY (*striking a pose*)
Well, I had talent.

ADELE (*maliciously*)
So they tell me!

SALLY (*incensed*) Oh!

ADELE
(*changing her tone, pleading*)
Will you please give me a chance?

SALLY
Alright, alright. I'll keep your pathetic little secret, for my own sake, if not for yours, but . . .

FALKE (*entering*)
Oh, ladies, how nice to see you. Well, well—

(*to Adele*)
Congratulations on your new career!

ADELE (*stupefied*)

Career?

FALKE (*to Sally*)

Excuse me, Miss Sally.

(*to Adele*)

Yes, you are making your debut in a starring role in a new play.

ADELE

My debut? When?

FALKE

Any minute now. Let me be the one to introduce you. Oh, another thing: Your stage name is Tanya.

(*A fanfare is heard.*)

ADELE (*delighted*)

It is?

IVAN

(*appearing rear Center, announces in a booming voice*)

His Imperial Highness, Prince Alexander, Alexandrovitch, Alexandrovsky, Petrovich, Ivanovsky *Orlofsky!*

(*All guests bow low, toward rear.*)

ORLOFSKY

(*enters from S.L. front, blasé, melancholic, with a strong Russian accent*)

Somebodjy having a parrty?

FALKE

Ssh, the prince is coming!

ORLOFSKY

Oh, parrdon me.

(*bows with the others*)

FALKE

(*realizing the prince's presence*)

Your Highness.

ORLOFSKY

I am your Highness?

FALKE

Yes, your Highness.

ORLOFSKY

Ivan! Make a note of that.

(*to all*)

In that case, welcome, my good friends and honorred guests. You arre all here to enjoy yourselves. The gaming room, the ball room, the gardenia-festooned champagne baths—whatever is your pleasure. Take your choice. *Chacun à son goût.*

ADELE (*to Sally*)

What did he say?

SALLY

Chacun à son goût.

ADELE

What does that mean?

ORLOFSKY

Each to his own taste.

(*Sally curtseys, then Adele in an awkward manner.*)

(*Orlofsky bows equally stiffly to Adele.*)

FALKE

Ah, your Highness! How gracious of you to honor us with your presence. Tonight, I'm sure that you will laugh. I've planned a magnificent divertissement, in addition to the usual games, chemin de fer, Russian roulette, champagne, dancing girls and so forth. Tonight we're going to have a domestic comedy.

ORLOFSKY (*sighing*)

I've seen a domestic comedy.

FALKE

Ah, your Highness, not one like this. This one is real.

ORLOFSKY

What is the title of the piece?

FALKE (*animatedly*)

"The Revenge of the Bat." It's a sequel to "The Crime of the Butterfly."

ORLOFSKY (*disapproving*)

An orrnithological horror storry.

FALKE

Not quite. But you will see.

ORLOFSKY

Dear Falke, nyeverr in my life have I been so borred. Everything bores me. I cannot laugh. My billions arre my misfortune.

FALKE

I would be delighted to share your misfortune, your Highness.

ORLOFSKY

Make me laugh tonight, and I'll **give** you a beautiful medal.

FALKE

Agreed. You gave me *carte blanche,* and I have taken great pains to prepare my little dramatic joke.

ADELE

(crossing with Sally from S.R. to rear)

I can't get over it! How does he make all his money?

SALLY

He does not make it, he just spends it.

FALKE

(stopping Sally and Adele)

Your Highness, may I present Mlle. Sally of the ballet?

(Sally curtseys.)

ORLOFSKY

(looking at Sally through his monocle)

Haven't I seen you somewherre beforre?

SALLY *(flattered)*

Why, of course, your Highness!

FALKE

She's one of your dancing girls.

ORLOFSKY

Ivan! Make a note of that.

(to Falke)

But who's the otherr one? I would like to meet *her!*

FALKE

Her sister Tanya, the rising young actress.

ORLOFSKY

Hm. I predict she will go far.

FALKE

Ah yes, your Highness, as far as you like.

ORLOFSKY *(to Adele)*

So you're an actress?

FALKE

(seeing Adele's embarrassment)

And what an actress!

ADELE *(bursting out)*

Oh, your Highness, this is all so delightful, your party is so delightful and your palace is so delightful and you're so delightful and how are you?

ORLOFSKY *(dryly)*

I'm bored.

FALKE

Your Highness, I see that your guests are enjoying themselves in the gambling room. Wouldn't you like to join them?

ORLOFSKY

Indeed not! I might win, by chance, and that would bore me. But perhaps you ladies would like to test my luck with the contents of this wallet.

(hands them his full wallet)

ADELE and SALLY

Oh!

(They leave, giggling, S.R.)

ORLOFSKY

Now tell me more about your play, Falke.

FALKE

Your Highness must allow me the pleasure of surprising him. But for the moment, I might say that Mlle. Tanya is the chambermaid of our hero.

ORLOFSKY *(unimpressed)*

I'm bored.

IVAN

(in a booming voice, announcing)

Marquis Renard!

FALKE

And here is our hero in person!

EISENSTEIN

(entering animatedly, from S.L., addressing Falke)

Ah, there you are. I came as fast as I could. Where are they?

FALKE

Who?

EISENSTEIN

Those lovely, lovely ladies you promised me.

FALKE

Some are in the champagne baths.

(Eisenstein wants to leave S.R.)

But wait, you can join them later. First let me present you to our host.

EISENSTEIN

Prince Orlofsky?

(bows to Orlofsky)

ORLOFSKY

Marquis, I am delighted to meet you.

EISENSTEIN

It is an honor, your Highness.

ORLOFSKY

You are welcome here. Welcome to spend the night exactly as you please.

EISENSTEIN

Exactly as I please? Well . . .

(starts for S.L.)

ORLOFSKY

Ivan!

(to Eisenstein)

Will you do me the honor of drinking a glass of champagne with me?

EISENSTEIN

(reluctantly, but politely)

It will be a pleasure.

(Ivan brings a tray with glasses and champagne.)

ORLOFSKY

And now, let me acquaint you with the rules of my house. Each to his own taste. *Chacun à son goût.*

No. 7. COUPLETS

ORLOFSKY

From time to time I entertain,
I am the perfect host.
My guests drink vodka and champagne,
And do what they like the most.
Each one is free to have his fun,
My house is freedom hall.
In other words to coin a pun:
It is a free-for-all.
You're free to go and free to come.
You're free to go astray;
I want you to enjoy yourself,
But don't get in my way!
And if it does not suit you,
That, too, is up to you.
We Russians have a motto:
Chacun à son goût.

There's not a sight I have not seen,
No place I have not been.
There's not a thing beneath the sun,
I haven't heard or done.
There's not a price I cannot pay
No sum I can't afford,
But I have never found a way
To keep from getting bored.
I do not care for music much,
Not even Johann Strauss,
The operetta I hate most
Is called "The Fledermaus,"
If you don't like it either,

You know what you can do:
Get up and leave the theatre,
Chacun à son goût.

(after applause, encore)

Like ev'ry other Russian Prince
I've had my ups and downs,
I've seen New York, Madrid and Linz
And lots and other towns.
I'm bored by Paris in the spring,
By London in the fall,
And Moscow is discouraging
Most any time at all.
Tonight I tell you face to face,
You win the big award,
For (..........)* is the only place
Where I am never bored.
But if you do not like me,
You know what you can do,
There's always television,
Chacun à son goût.

(returning with Falke after the applause)

Falke, now tell me, what is so novel about this hero of yours?

FALKE

Wait until you meet his wife. I've invited her also.

ORLOFSKY

And that is supposed to make me laugh?

FALKE

He's not a marquis, and his wife thinks he's in jail. You see, it gets better and better!

ORLOFSKY

It better!

ADELE

(entering with Sally, excitedly, without noticing the prince)

It's all your fault. I told you not to play this number! You're always showing off!

(seeing Orlofsky, meekly)

Your Highness, here's your wallet. It's the only thing we didn't lose.

ORLOFSKY

Think nothing of it. Ivan!

(Ivan steps up quickly, Orlofsky motions to him, Ivan hands him a full wallet, which Orlofsky passes on to Adele. Handing the empty wallet to Ivan:)

Have this one refilled!

(Eisenstein enters from S.L., not noticing Adele.)

* Insert name of the town where performance is given.

FALKE

Marquis, may I present Mlle. Tanya,
the rising young actress?

EISENSTEIN and ADELE

(recognizing each other, simul-
taneously, under their breath)

My master!
Adele!

(embarrassed silence)

FALKE *(to Adele, softly)*

This is your debut. Make the most of it.

ORLOFSKY

Marquis, Mlle. Tanya seems to have
impressed you beyond words.

EISENSTEIN

Oh, no—it's not that—only—the resemblance—

ORLOFSKY

Resemblance?

EISENSTEIN *(to Adele)*

Mlle. Tanya, how long have you been
an actress?

ADELE

About as long as you've been a marquis!

EISENSTEIN

That face! That resemblance!

ADELE

To whom, Marquis?

EISENSTEIN

You look just like a chambermaid I
know.

ADELE

(pretending to be shocked)

A chambermaid! Well, I like that! I've
never been so insulted in all my life.

FALKE *(calling the guests)*

Ladies! Gentlemen!

No. 8. ENSEMBLE AND LAUGHING SONG

ORLOFSKY

My friends, your kind attention!
Don't miss this comic scene!

FALKE

We need your intervention!

ALL

What's up! What does he mean?

ORLOFSKY

See this delightful lady,
Marquis Renard takes her for . . .
No, I can't believe it . . .

ALL

For what then?

FALKE

Take a guess!

ADELE

He takes me for a chambermaid
On holiday parade.

CHORUS

Hahaha!
He's trying to be funny!

ORLOFSKY

Marquis, you are most impolite,
You surely are mistaken!
How impolite!

CHORUS

How impolite!

EISENSTEIN

The likeness was a shock to me!

ALL

How impolite!

EISENSTEIN

I could have sworn that it was she!

ADELE

My dear Marquis,
It seems to me
You should display more tact!
Where a lady goes,
What a lady shows,
Is how she proves the fact.
My taste is too fine and too chic,
My waist has a line too unique,
My talk is so dramatic
My walk aristocratic!
What chambermaid you know
Could have so much to show?
Instead of putting on such airs
Why don't you mind your own affairs?
It's too funny,—ha, ha, ha—
Please excuse me,—ha, ha, ha—
I can't help it,—ha, ha, ha!
You amuse me,—ha, ha, ha, ha, ha,
  ha, ha!
Just look at me
And you'll agree
There's more than meets the eye.
Where a lady's been,
Where a lady's seen,
Are proofs that never lie.
Could I be at home in this room,
If I were at home with a broom?

The way I lift an eyebrow,
Is typically high-brow!
What chambermaid you know
Could have so much to show?
You might as well admit, Marquis,
You owe me an apology.
It's too funny, ha, ha, ha, etc.

EISENSTEIN

My humblest apologies, Miss Tanya!
There never was an actress like you!

ADELE

Nor a marquis like you, Marquis!

IVAN (announcing)

Chevalier Chagrin!!

FALKE (to Orlofsky)

Chevalier Chagrin. *Nom de plume,*
shall we say, for Prison Warden
Frank.

ORLOFSKY

I begin to follow you.

FRANK

(entering from S.L. rear)

Good evening, Falke.

FALKE

I am happy you have arrived, Chevalier. May I present our host, Prince
Orlofsky?

FRANK (flattered, bowing low)

Oh, Prince!

ORLOFSKY

Welcome, Chevalier. And may I present
a fellow Frenchman, Marquis Renard? I'm sure you will enjoy talking
your native language.
(*Eisenstein and Frank move away from
each other, in embarrassment.*)

EISENSTEIN (hesitating)

Oui, of course, but we don't wish to be
impolite.

ORLOFSKY

Pas de tout, all my guests are multi-
lingual.
(*Guests murmur approval in various
languages.*)

EISENSTEIN

That too—
(*stammering*)
Chevalier—*sa-voir faire?*

FRANK

(*searching his memory*)

Croix de guerre?

EISENSTEIN

(*moving a little toward Frank*)

Courage—

FRANK

(*moving a little toward Eisenstein*)

Bon voyage—

EISENSTEIN

Ah, oui!

FRANK

Paris!

EISENSTEIN

Amour!

FRANK

Toujours!

EISENSTEIN

La bonne chance!

FRANK and EISENSTEIN

Vive la France!
(*They embrace, French style.*)

ALL GUESTS

Vive la France!

ORLOFSKY (to Falke)

Men of few words, *n'est-ce pas?*

FALKE

Few, but well chosen.

EISENSTEIN

(*now quite at ease*)

Chevalier — have you been in town
long?

FRANK (same)

No, I just arrived this evening.

FALKE

Then you gentlemen haven't met before?

EISENSTEIN

No, I'm sorry to say.

FRANK

I seldom appear in public—I am a
great lover of—
(*crossing his fists*)
closed circles. In the future however—

FALKE

You will indubitably see a great deal of
each other.

EISENSTEIN

We shall become inseparable.

FALKE

I am sure you will.
(*to all*)
But now, my friends, I wish to ask your
discretion and cooperation. The
Prince is expecting an important
guest, a Hungarian countess.

EISENSTEIN

Oh, is she pretty?

FALKE

She is glorious. She is very anxious to join our charming company, but she insists upon remaining incognito. She is going to wear a mask.

FRANK (*forgetting himself*)

Oh, that's nothing. Lots of people come to my place wearing a mask.

EISENSTEIN

I imagine she's married?

FALKE

Oh yes, to a man who is so jealous that he would like to carry her around in his wallet, if he could.

EISENSTEIN

The man must be a jackass!

FALKE

He is. Although her husband is away for a week on a—"secret mission," she is nevertheless careful to come to this party masked.

FRANK

Not *all* covered up?

FALKE

Only partially, I feel sure. But I've assured her that everyone will respect her wishes.

EISENSTEIN and FRANK

You can count on us!

FALKE

Thank you! And now, may I propose a promenade in the garden until supper is served?

FRANK

A superb idea! Come, Marquis, let's try our luck.

EISENSTEIN

Yes, let's. I have a little toy here that I'd like to try my luck with.

(*They exit to the garden.*)

ORLOFSKY (*to Falke*)

Now what, Falke?

IVAN (*announcing*)

Countess Hunyani!

FALKE

We have arrived at the crucial moment. Here she is.

ORLOFSKY

Who?

FALKE

Eisenstein's wife.

(*Rosalinda appears S.C. in gorgeous ball-gown, wearing a wig, a mask and a feather fan.*)

ORLOFSKY

Most gracious lady! Welcome to our humble palace.

ROSALINDA

(*in a disguised voice, with Hungarian accent*)

Thank you, your Highness.

ORLOFSKY

Doctor Falke tells me that you are from Hungary?

ROSALINDA (*as before*)

Very much from Hungary.

ORLOFSKY

For the moment I shall leave you in the best of hands. May I wish you a charming and interesting evening.

(*bows and exits S.R.*)

ROSALINDA

(*alone with Falke, in a natural voice*)

Now tell me, Falke, is it really true what you wrote in your letter?

FALKE

Only too true, dear lady. A glance into the garden will convince you. Look at your husband, serving his sentence!

ROSALINDA

(*looking toward the garden*)

My husband! With all those girls! Why it's positively scandalous the way he's behaving! And who is that? Why, she looks exactly like my chambermaid!

FALKE

It *is* your chambermaid — your own Adele.

ROSALINDA

(*almost losing her temper*)

Dying aunt! Indeed! I have just the medicine for her!

FALKE (*restraining her*)

Not tonight, my lady, I beg you! Careful, she's coming back!

(*Adele enters, in animated conversation with a gentleman.*)

FALKE

Countess, may I present Mlle. Tanya, the rising young actress?

ROSALINDA (*resuming her accent*)

An actress! Have I ever seen you on the stage?

ADELE

Up to now I've only played maid's parts.

ROSALINDA

Oh, vat a lovely, lovely gown you're vearingg.

ADELE (*blasé*)

You like it? Just an old rag I picked up. (*Exit S.L.*)

ROSALINDA

(*flaring up, with natural voice*)

My dress! *My* dress!

FALKE

Careful, *he's* coming back!

EISENSTEIN

(*entering S.R. rear, dangling his watch, while several girls follow him, giggling*)

One at a time, ladies, don't crowd!

FRANK

(*entering after them, with two girls on his arms*)

You seem to be having the time of your life with that watch, Marquis!

EISENSTEIN

It never lost a minute, or a girl.

(*noticing Rosalinda*)

Oh—isn't she ravishing!

(*leaving the girls and approaching Rosalinda*)

Madame, may I take the liberty of presenting myself. I'm Marquis Renard.

ROSALINDA (*with accent*)

And I am the Countess Hunyani!

FALKE

Countess, this is a dear and charming friend of mine whom I've been anxious to introduce to you.

ROSALINDA

You mean *this* Marquis?

(*stabs Eisenstein a little with her fan*)

FALKE

Yes, Marquis Renard.

(*Eisenstein dangles his watch by the chain.*)

ROSALINDA

Ah, vat a charrmingg vatch!

EISENSTEIN

Yes, isn't it?

FALKE

(*noticing that Eisenstein would like to be left alone with Rosalinda*)

If you'll excuse me, I shall go and greet some friends.

(*to Eisenstein*)

Enjoy yourself!

(*Exit S.R. rear.*)

ROSALINDA

Vere does one buy such prretty vatches?

EISENSTEIN

One doesn't. It's a priceless family heirloom.

ROSALINDA

A pity. I vould love to have one like it.

EISENSTEIN

Would you like to know what time it is?

ROSALINDA (*with meaning*)

I know exactly vat time it is. But tell me, Marrquis, are you married?

EISENSTEIN

Heavens, no! Whatever gave you that idea?

ROSALINDA

Oh, just a feminine intuition.

EISENSTEIN

Dear lady, allow me a question. Wouldn't you be more comfortable if you were to take off your mask?

ROSALINDA

Not tonight, but tomorrow morrningg.

EISENSTEIN

But tomorrow will be too late!

ROSALINDA

Too late?

EISENSTEIN

Yes. Tomorrow morning I shall be in conference.

ROSALINDA

In conference?

EISENSTEIN

Yes. A private one—no admittance to the public.

ROSALINDA

Vat a shame. You know, Marquis, your vatch is just adorable.

EISENSTEIN

If you will unmask for me, I might even weaken and present you with it.

ROSALINDA

My husband vill be mad about it!

EISENSTEIN

The devil with your husband!

ROSALINDA

How rright you are!

No. 9. DUET

EISENSTEIN (*to himself*)

How engaging, how exciting,
How adorably inviting!
Such a flower I could shower
With my kisses here and now
If she only would allow.

ROSALINDA (*to herself*)

Masquerading, under cover,
He approaches me as lover.
Was a liar
Ever slyer!
Just you wait, dear Eisenstein,
I will make you toe the line.

EISENSTEIN

Like a fleeting, magic vision,
You may vanish from my sight!
Will you change your firm decision
And unmask for me tonight?

ROSALINDA

Please, my dear Marquis, don't ask me.
That's one thing I won't do.
I insist you don't unmask me.
I expect that much from you.
(*to herself*)
How he prances
And romances
While he boldly makes advances.
No suspicion,
Premonition,
Warns him who resists his charms.
In a minute he'll discover,
This philand'ring would-be lover,
How completely he has fallen in my trap.

EISENSTEIN (*to himself*)

From her glances
And advances
I have chances,
I am sure.
If I try and persist,
How can she resist?
In a minute I'll discover,
Yes, I will see whether she can resist,
Or will fall into my trap.

ROSALINDA

(*with weak voice, placing her hand upon her heart and staggering to the couch*)

Ah, my heart is weak and tender,
And my brain begins to spin.

EISENSTEIN

(*observing her triumphantly*)

Ah, she's going to surrender,
Pretty soon she will give in.

ROSALINDA

Ah, my pulse is beating wildly,
Throbbing on, tick, tock, tick, tock!
Could we measure its pulsations
By your precious little clock?

EISENSTEIN

That's just what I want to say!

ROSALINDA

Let us count them right away.

BOTH

Yes, let us count,
Let us count them right away.

EISENSTEIN

One, two, three, four,

ROSALINDA

Five, six, sev'n, nine,

EISENSTEIN

No, that's not in line,
For after seven there is eight.

ROSALINDA

I thought perhaps that I was late,
Let's change positions.

EISENSTEIN

Change them? How?

ROSALINDA

You count the beats of my heart,
And I the ticking of your watch,
And let us start from the start.
(*She takes watch and chain, which Eisenstein hands her.*)
Now let us count without delay.

EISENSTEIN

Yes, right away.

BOTH

One, two, three, four, five, six, sev'n, eight,
Nine, ten, 'lev'n, twelve, thirteen, fourteen,

ROSALINDA

Fifteen, sixteen, sev'nteen, eighteen,
Nineteen, twenty, thirty, forty, fifty,
Sixty, eighty, hundred.

EISENSTEIN

Hop, hop, hop, on without a stop!
Six hundred and nine!

ROSALINDA

My goodness, we can't be that far!

EISENSTEIN

Oh yes, indeed we are,
Half a million beats at least!

ROSALINDA

No, no, no!
That is a little too fantastic!

EISENSTEIN

My figures are a bit elastic.

ROSALINDA

You'll never count another heartbeat.

EISENSTEIN

She took my watch away from me,
How unkind!

ROSALINDA

I thank you sincerely!

EISENSTEIN

If you don't mind?

ROSALINDA

I'll cherish it dearly.

EISENSTEIN

She outwitted all my guesses
And my watch she now possesses.
This flirtation cost me dearly,
I disgraced myself severely.
(grasping for the watch)
Ah, lovely watch, oh, give it back,
Please give it back!
I disgraced myself severely.
Ah, dearest watch,
If I only had you back.
Please give it back.
This flirtation cost me dearly,
I disgraced myself severely!
And my watch has gone to waste,
Ah, I am disgraced. Poor me!

FALKE

(entering, with several guests. Other guests enter from all sides.)

My friends, the Prince's dancers have prepared a little divertissement for your entertainment.

BALLET SEQUENCE
(usually one of the famous Strauss waltzes)

ADELE

(entering with Sally, pointing out Rosalinda)

That's the mysterious countess I was telling you about!

SALLY

I certainly would like to see her face!

OTHER GUESTS

So would I! So would I!

ADELE

Come on, let's persuade her to unmask.

ALL

Yes, please!

ORLOFSKY

Wait, my friends, you are breaking the agreement! In my house, every lady has the right to coverr and uncoverr as much as she likes.

ADELE

I wonder if she's really Hungarian.

FALKE

She *is* Hungarian.

SALLY

But can she prove it?

ROSALINDA

The music will prove it. The melodies of my homeland wil speak for me!

No. 10. Czardas

ROSALINDA

Voice of my homeland,
Nostalgic, enthralling,
I hear you calling
And tears fill my eyes.
Dreaming, I hear your plaintive sighing,
And I'm lonely for you,
My native skies.
O homeland I hold so dear,

Where sunlight is golden and clear,
Where green forests tower
And fields are in flower,
O land that I love and revere.
Never, oh never your image will fade
From my memory,
Your beloved name!
Wherever I may wander, ah—
Far, ah—as lonely years go by,
To you my thoughts will fly,
Till the day I die!
O homeland I hold so dear, etc.

Fiery evening sky,
Spirits are soaring high.
Friends all gather round,
Hear the czardas sound.
Lovely gypsy girl,
Come, dance the merry whirl;
Child of Romany,
Give your heart to me!
Fiddles are ringing—
Hey-ya!

Wildly singing, hey-ya-ya!
Twirling round and round,
Stamping the dusty ground,
Dance the night away
Till the break of day.
Lads and lasses,
Lift your glasses,
Pass the bottles fast from hand to hand!
Drown your sorrow
Till tomorrow.
Raise a toast to the fatherland! Ha!
Fiery evening sky,
Spirits are soaring high.
Friends all gather round,
Hear the czardas sound.
Lalalala.

(*After the number, everybody applauds.*)

EISENSTEIN

She is typically Hungarian.

ORLOFSKY

And now, my friends, I propose a toast
to our lovely guest!

FALKE

A toast to her wonderful music!

EISENSTEIN

And a toast—a toast to the life of our
party—to King Champagne!

No. 11. FINALE

ORLOFSKY

Champagne's delicious bubbles
Tra la, la la la la la la

Scatter all our troubles
Tra la, la la la la la la
It mellows politicians
And betters world conditions.
All diplomats and rulers
Should keep it in their coolers!

EISENSTEIN

Champagne is so majestic
Tra la, la la la la la la
Foreign and domestic
Tra la, la la la la la la
It makes the world we live in
A better place to give in!
All "good and jolly fellers"
Should keep it in their cellars!

ADELE

Champagne is so romantic!
Tra la, la la la la la la
Glorious and gigantic!
Tra la, la la la la la la
It makes the world look thrilling
And men become more willing!
All girls who long for sables
Should keep it on their tables!

ALL

We toast Champagne,
The essence of the essence,
The King of Effervescence!
A toast! A toast! A toast!
His Majesty we celebrate, celebrate,
Long and late!
Joyously together
We toast Champagne the Great!

EISENSTEIN

My Chevalier, O *bon ami!*

FRANK

Merci, merci, merci!
Another little drink, Marquis!

EISENSTEIN

Oui oui, oui oui, oui oui!

FALKE

That's enough of French for today!

EISENSTEIN, FRANK

Touché, touché, touché!

ROSALINDA, ADELE, ORLOFSKY, SALLY

Ha, ha, ha!

FALKE

Friends, gather near,
Here's my idea!
Let us hear!

ALL

FALKE

I see that happy couples are meeting,
That many hearts with true love are
  beating;
So why not continue in this happy
  mood
And sing to love and brotherhood?

ORLOFSKY

I agree most heartily, that's good!

ALL

Let us sing to love and brotherhood!

EISENSTEIN

You too, lovely lady, must be there.

ROSALINDA

When all are kissing
I can't be missing.

FALKE

Let's lift our glasses and drink again,
And ev'rybody join the refrain.
Sing to love, love we never knew be-
  fore,
May it flourish and bloom forevermore.
Sing to love, everlasting happiness,
Let us all be friends together,
For eternity,
A fraternity
Of companions, friends, and lovers.
First a kiss,
Then one more,
You, you, and always you!
You kiss me,
I kiss you,
Only you, only you.
(One after the other joins in.)
You and I, I and you
La la la la la la
La la la la la la la la.

ORLOFSKY

Enough my friends, enough!
You may cease this merry dance,
With jubilant singing,
Let glasses be clinging,
And we ourselves begin the dance.

CHORUS

Yes, yes, a dance, a rollicking dance,
Let's all begin to dance!
On with the dance, with the dance!
Let's all begin to dance!
(All begin to waltz.)

ALL

Ah, happy day of divine delight!
Love and champagne banish care from
  sight.
Could we live on as we do tonight,
Life would forever be gay and bright.
(Eisenstein and Frank, waltzing, meet.)

EISENSTEIN

(supporting himself on Frank)
You are all I have on earth!

FRANK

You are my only salvation.

ROSALINDA, ORLOFSKY, FALKE

When you meet in jail again,
How funny a situation!

SOLI, CHORUS

Ah, happy day of divine delight! etc.

FRANK (to Eisenstein)

Brother, brother, my watch is slow;
Tell me what time it is.

EISENSTEIN

(looking for his watch)
Brother, mine also does not go,
For it is already gone.
    (to Rosalinda)
Charming lady,
I am asking,
Would you mind unmasking,
Let me see whom I adore,
And who stole my watch before?

ROSALINDA

(grasping his hand, drawing him
    forward confidentially)
My friend do not ask what I conceal,
The shock you would get would make
  you reel.

EISENSTEIN

Huhuhuhuhuh! You are too cruel!

ADELE, ORLOFSKY, SALLY

Hahahaha, she is no fool,
Indeed, she's nobody's fool!

CHORUS, SOLI

Indeed, she's nobody's fool!

ADELE

Are you afraid?
Then go ahead!

CHORUS

Go ahead.

SALLY

Perhaps she will weaken, if you are
  clever.

EISENSTEIN

It has to be now or never.
    (to Rosalinda)
Darling, do not hide from me.

ROSALINDA
There's a freckle on my nose,
Therefore I must hide my face.

EISENSTEIN
Such a freckle cannot be!

OTHERS
That disturbs him no degree.

EISENSTEIN
No, your face I have to see!

OTHERS
Yes, her face he has to see!
(*Eisenstein pursues Rosalinda.*)
(*The clock strikes.*)

EISENSTEIN, FRANK (*counting*)
One, two, three, four, five, six!

EISENSTEIN (*startled*)
Where's my hat? Where's my coat?
It is very late!

FRANK (*likewise*)
Where's my hat? Where's my coat?
It is very late!

SOLI, CHORUS
Bring his hat! Bring his coat,
Oh don't make him wait!

EISENSTEIN
They are looking for me!

FRANK
And I know where I should be!

BOTH
Where's my hat? Where's my coat?
Oh give me my coat!
(*Servants bring assorted coats and hats
which do not fit.*)

SOLI, CHORUS
Bring his coat! Bring his hat! Bring
his coat! Hahaha!
Bring his hat! Oh bring him his coat!
Hahaha!

FRANK (*leaning on Eisenstein*)
Dear Marquis, I hope you will call on
me.

EISENSTEIN
Yes, indeed, the moment my time is
free.

BOTH
Let's say goodbye.

SOLI
Goodbye! Haha!

ALL
Ah, happy day of divine delight! etc.
(*Eisenstein and Frank, dancing the last
tempo, move, staggering, arm in arm,
toward the background. They are
surrounded by the dancers, while the
curtain falls.*)

ACT THREE

The Jail.

*In center rear a grilled gate, leading to
the prison cells. The center bars of
the grill are made of rubber. At S.R.
rear an arch, leading to the outside.
Front L. a desk with a chair and a
bench in front of it. A ledger on the
desk. A window with iron bars S.L.
rear.*

It is early morning.

*Alfred is heard singing loudly, the
Miserere from Trovatore.*

FROSCH
(*Sweeping the floor with a broom. He
is in a state of happy drunkenness.
A large key is hanging on a chain
from his neck.*)
QUIET! Quiet!
(*Alfred stops singing.*)
Music, music, all day long. And all
night too! Where else could you find
a jail with so much culture! That
calls for a drink!
(*He takes a bottle from his pocket and
takes a drink.*)
Ah, that's good!
(*Alfred sings again, an aria from
Rigoletto or Traviata.*)
Quiet! Quiet! Quiet! That fellow in
No. 12 sings opera in fifteen different
languages. There ought to be a law
against singing opera. I think I'll look
it up.
(*goes to the ledger, opens it and finds
a large bottle in it, drinks*)
Ah, I feel better. What a nice prison
this is. So sociable! The most wonderful little jail in the world.
(*kisses the wall*)
Love that jail! Well, I suppose, I'd better go to work. I wonder what I did
with my key?

(He looks in all his pockets, finally discovers it hanging around his neck.)

Oh, there it is. If it had been a snake, it would have bitten me.

(suddenly, terrified)

Snake-bite!

(He rushes to the desk, grabs the bottle and drinks frantically.)

That was a narrow escape!

(Goes to the gate, brushes against the bars. A tone is heard.)

(Harp in orchestra. He plucks first one tone, then another, finally a few chords, at last glissandos.)

Never took a lesson in my life!

(Exits.)

No. 13. MELODRAMA

(Frank appears, his overcoat awry, his hat pressed down deep over his eyes. He staggers and tries in vain to walk steadily. Coming forward, he takes off his hat and tosses it into a corner. He begins quietly to move in time to the music and whistles to himself. He becomes more and more lively and waltzes with his half-removed overcoat. Suddenly he stops . . . remembering where he is, he pulls himself together, makes an effort to be serious and tries again to take off his overcoat . . . finally succeeding. His high spirits gain the upper hand again. He thinks he is in the ballroom, makes several bows, and mumbles: "Tanya, come here . . . Sally, too! I like you!" He turns toward the other side and speaks with a heavy tongue: "Marquis, give me your hand, be my friend." Sings first softly, humming to himself, then increasingly louder. Looks around, frightened, to see if anyone has heard him and tries to appear steady on his feet. He notices the tea-things on the table in the back and goes toward them. He carries them, staggering and with great effort, to the table in the foreground, lights the oil lamp after a few comic attempts. He is very warm. He fans himself and drinks a glass of water. Sinks exhausted into a chair, grasps a newspaper and tries to read, but his thoughts still fly to the dance. He whistles, falling asleep. Lets the newspaper fall and goes to sleep.)

FROSCH *(re-enters)*

I wonder where the warden is.

(notices the warden's top hat on the floor)

There's the top of him. I wonder where the rest of him is.

(He tries to hang the hat up; since there is no hook, it falls to the floor. He takes a piece of chalk out of his pocket, draws a hook on the wall. The hat stays. He discovers the warden, goes to him, shouts:)

Warden! Warden!

FRANK *(startled)*

Where am I?

FROSCH

In jail.

FRANK

What put me in jail?

FROSCH

Dirty politics. Officer Frosch reporting.

(salutes, loses balance, falls down some distance from Frank)

How did you get over there?

FRANK

How did *you* get over *there?* Bring yourself over here.

FROSCH

(makes an effort, moves a bit)

Is that better?

FRANK

Oh, will you stand still?

FROSCH *(staggering forward)*

I'm as steady as the rock of Gibraltar.

FRANK

Well, Frosch, what's new?

FROSCH

Nothing, warden. Only that No. 12 is asking for a lawyer.

FRANK

No. 12? That's Eisenstein, isn't it? As far as I am concerned, he's entitled to a lawyer.

FROSCH

I sent for Mr. Blind, to keep him quiet.

(Alfred is heard singing again.)

Quiet, quiet, quiet!!!

FRANK

Have you anything else to report?

FROSCH

Yes sir!—Nothing that I can remember.

FRANK

Then sit down and tell me whether you like this place. Everything comfortable? Everything satisfactory?

FROSCH

(*sitting down next to Frank, very palsy*)

I tell you, warden, I was just saying to myself today, it's the best little old jail I've ever seen, absolutely *gemuetlich* . . .

(*The bell rings.*)

FRANK

There's the bell.

FROSCH

Bell? Are you hearing them too?

FRANK

Go look and see who's there.

FROSCH (*staggering*)

Way over there?

FRANK

Yes, and hurry!

FROSCH

With the utmost dispatch.

(*staggers off slowly, S.R. rear*)
(*coming back*)

There are two ladies at the door.

FRANK

Two ladies?

FROSCH

Maybe only one. They say they want to see a Mr. Chandelier Chagrin.

FRANK

Chandelier Chagrin? We haven't arrested anyone by that name.

FROSCH

She says her name is Mlle. Tan-ya.

FRANK (*excited*)

Tanya! Go let her in. I'll be right back. (*exits hurriedly S.L.*)

FROSCH

(*while going to open, S.R. rear*)

I wonder if that's her real name or merely a *pomme-de-terre.*

SALLY AND ADELE

(*enter, with Frosch S.R.*)

Oh, isn't this a wonderful place, etc. . . .

ADELE

I wonder what all those bars are on the window?

FRANK

That's to keep the riff-raff out.

SALLY (*to Adele*)

Did you notice all the guards outside?

ADELE

That's probably to guard the jewels.

SALLY

(*looking around, noticing the numbers on the prison cells*)

Imagine! A house with thirteen guestrooms!

ADELE

He must be very wealthy!

(*Frank comes back from S.L.*)

SALLY AND ADELE

(*crowding Frank*)

Oh there he is, the dear . . . (ad lib)

FRANK

Stop it, stop it! What are you doing here?

SALLY

Did you forget all your promises?

FRANK (*worried*)

Promises? What did I say?

ADELE

You said we should come and live with you. That you had the biggest house in town.

FROSCH

You are mistaken. He means the BIG house in town.

ADELE

And we could be your honored guests.

FRANK

Now, ladies, only criminals come here.

ADELE

I am a criminal, and I came here to confess.

FRANK

Confess?

ADELE

You see, I'm not what I appear to be.

SALLY

What my sister means is that she isn't
an actress. In your position you could
easily help her.

ADELE

What I'm trying to tell you is—I am a
chambermaid.

FRANK

A chambermaid?

ADELE

Yes, I am. And Mr. von Eisenstein is
my master.

FRANK

Von Eisenstein?

ADELE

Yes. And I thought that maybe, since
you had the opportunity, you would
put in a good word for me with him.

FRANK

About what?

ADELE

He knows that I went to Prince Orlofsky's party in his wife's dress—

SALLY

—She borrowed without her permission.

FRANK

Oh, your mistress will dismiss you on
the spot!

SALLY

Adele dismissed herself anyway.

ADELE

To tell the truth, I've decided to let
myself be developed
        (*in an affected voice*)
for the theatre.

FRANK

(*looking admiringly at Adele's figure*)
A very natural development. But have
you any talent?

ADELE

(*while music No. 14 starts*)
Have I? Just let me show you.

No. 14. AUDITION SONG

ADELE

Ever since I was a baby
I always was hoping that maybe
As soon as I got to the age,
I'd get my big chance on the stage.

You never saw such a prodigy
As up and as coming as me.
You should see how I do
As the shy *ingénue:*
I sing and dance and wave my fan,
And in the end I get my man.
He says to me: "Let's take a walk."
He holds my hand, we hardly talk.
We wander slowly through the park.
The lights fade out, the stage is dark.
La la la la la la la la, etc.
If you saw the way
I can act and play,
The fact is absolutely clear,
That a girl like me, a girl like me,
Was born for a stage career!
When I play Madame Pompadour
I do it with *"l'amour, l'amour."*
Smiling here, and greeting there,
I run, ah!, each little state affair.
I have a mink and an ermine of my
        own.
I'm the power behind the throne.
Proud and stately, dignified, serene,
I am ev'ry inch a queen!
La la la la la la la, etc.
If you saw the way
I can act and play,
The fact is absolutely clear
That a girl like me, a girl like me,
Was born for a stage career!
I play a young Parisian wife, ah!
Who's rather bored with married life,
        ah!
My husband is an old Marquis, ah, ah!
Who cannot quite keep up with me, ah!
I meet a handsome count one day.
We fall in love and run away.
In time the count betrays me, too,
Oh Lord, I don't know what to do! Ah!
Act III: my loving husband calls, ah!
I shoot them both, the curtain falls, ah,
        yes!

(*After applause, bell rings.*)

FROSCH

There's the bell, warden.

FRANK

Who can that be, so early in the morning?

FROSCH

Maybe it's the prison inspectors!

FRANK (*scared*)

Inspectors? Oh! Take these ladies into
No. 13 and see that they fill out the
proper forms.

FROSCH

(*while escorting them through the gate S. Ctr.*)

Those forms don't need any filling out. This way, ladies, this way.

(*Exit through gate.*)

(*Bell rings.*)

FRANK (*alone*)

Alright, alright! Someone is dying to get in when everybody else is dying to get out.

(*goes to open S.R.*)

EISENSTEIN

(*entering, with Frank*)

Chevalier! What are you doing here?

FRANK

I belong here!

EISENSTEIN (*jokingly*)

I suspected that the minute I saw you. I can always spot the criminal type. What happened, Chevalier, did they arrest you for disturbing the peace? Come on. Tell me!

FRANK

It so happens, my friend, that I'm the warden of this prison.

EISENSTEIN

I don't believe it.

FRANK

So you don't believe that I'm the warden of this prison?

(*calls loudly*)

Frosch!

FROSCH (*enters*)

You rang, Sir?

FRANK

No, I shouted!

FROSCH

It must be your bell-like tone.

FRANK

Seize that man.

FROSCH

Delighted. Sir, you are about to be seized.

(*He approaches Eisenstein, misses him, and passes him.*)

Where did he go? Ah, there you are! Trying to get away?

(*He seizes Eisenstein, after an effort.*)

FRANK

You can let him go now. It was just a joke.

FROSCH

Very, very funny! We are not amused.

FRANK

You may go now.

FROSCH

(*disappointed, exit S.R. rear*)

Just let me know if he gets obstreperous.

FRANK

Well, what do you say now, Marquis? Have I convinced you?

EISENSTEIN

Stop calling me "Marquis." I'm not a marquis. My name is Eisenstein, and I've come to serve my eight-day prison term. Now will you have the kindness to show me to my cell?

FRANK

Very clever, but unfortunately it does not work, because I can prove beyond the shadow of a doubt that you're *not* Eisenstein.

EISENSTEIN

That I would like to see.

(*Both sit down on the bench in front of the desk.*)

FRANK

It so happens that I arrested Eisenstein personally last night before Orlofsky's party.

EISENSTEIN

How nice for him. Where and when, please?

FRANK

Grinzingerstrasse 8, two flights up, on the dot of nine.

EISENSTEIN

Not bad. Did you find him at home?

FRANK

At home? Ho-ho-ho! Very much so. He was sitting in his dressing gown very comfortably, having supper with his wife.

EISENSTEIN

In *my* dressing gown with *my* wife?

FRANK

With *his* wife.

EISENSTEIN

But *his* wife is *my* wife.

FRANK

His wife is *his* wife!

EISENSTEIN

Then he must have two wives!
(*Both laugh.*)

FRANK

And I must say, never before have I
been more reluctant to do my duty.
It was positively touching, the way
they kissed each other—(*sniff*)—
goodbye!

EISENSTEIN

(*imitating mechanically*)

The way they kissed each other—
(*sniff*)—goodbye.

(*suddenly realizing*)

Where is this Eisenstein?

FRANK

In cell No. 12.

EISENSTEIN

I must see him immediately.

FRANK

I am terribly sorry, but no one is al-
lowed to visit prisoners without a
permit.

EISENSTEIN

Where do I get one?

FRANK

In the permit room. But you can't get
it today.

EISENSTEIN

I'll get it today if it takes me all week!
(*exits S.L.*)

FROSCH (*enters from S.R. rear*)

It's getting livelier and livelier in here.
There's another lady at the door.

FRANK

Another lady?

FROSCH

Yes.

FRANK

What does she look like?

FROSCH

Oh, she is absolutely beautiful. Her eyes
are like dark limpid pools—her hair
is like spun gold. Oh, she is a grande
dahme, and I don't give a dahm
about dames, no matter how
"grande" they are.

FRANK

Alright, have her wait in the waiting
room. Excuse me.
(*exits S.L.*)

FROSCH

What did you do?
(*exits S.R. rear*)

EISENSTEIN (*re-enters from S.C.*)

So there are two of us. And my alter
ego had supper with my wife. Oh,
Rosalinda, Rosalinda, after all I have
done for you, and the way I trusted
you! And here I stand without a permit to visit myself and have a few
violent words with me!

FROSCH

(*enters S.R., followed by Blind, wearing
cape, top-hat, glasses, holding a briefcase*)

Please wait right here, sir.
(*exits through C.*)

BLIND (*seeing Eisenstein*)

So you're here?

EISENSTEIN

That's none of your business. Besides I
am not only *here*, but *there* too.
Which reminds me: What are *you*
doing here, you justice-perverting
worm?

BLIND

How d-dare you speak to m-me like
that? You s-sent for me.

EISENSTEIN

I did?

BLIND

The messenger said most spe-ci-fi-cally
that you wanted me urgently.

EISENSTEIN

That's because Eisenstein is a jackass.

BLIND (*delighted*)

So you finally came around to m-my
point of view?

EISENSTEIN

Not this jackass, but the other jackass—
(*getting an idea*)
Give me your hat.
(*Blind does so, almost automatically.*)
And your spectacles.
(*same*)

And your cape—
 (*same*)
and your briefcase and your beard.

(*Blind refuses, runs away. Eisenstein
after him. A scream is heard offstage.*)

FROSCH
(*enters, shows Alfred in through gate
S. Center*)

Right this way.

ALFRED
I have a complaint.

FROSCH
You do?

ALFRED
Being falsely arrested. I don't mind that
so much. But how dare you keep me
all night in that drafty cell—
 (*cracks*)
cell—

(*vocalizes, notices a cold coming on*)

If anything happens to this glorious
voice of mine, I'll hold you personally
responsible.

FROSCH (*in a defying tone*)
And I accept the responsibility, and
personally guarantee you, that with
the continuous use of Dr. Frosch's
throat elixir, within six months you
will be with the Metropolitan . . .

(*hands him a whisky bottle, and starts
to leave*)

ALFRED (*flattered*)
Well!

FROSCH
(*before leaving entirely S.R. rear*)

. . . selling life insurance.

ALFRED (*offended*)
Sell—sell—
 (*cracks again, vocalizes*)

My glorious voice! And it is lost to the
world!

FROSCH
(*Ushering in Rosalinda. She wears a
hooded cape over her ball gown, and
no mask.*)

Right this way, most gracious lady.

ROSALINDA (*seeing Alfred*)
O Alfred, Alfred!

ALFRED (*with pathos*)
Heavens, can it be? I'm not deserted
after all. The comforting angel comes
to minister to me in my poor prison
cell—cell—cell—

(*sings a little; the cold is getting worse*)

ROSALINDA
Enough, Alfred. We have no time for
that now. Listen to me.

ALFRED
I listen.

ROSALINDA
You must leave this place at once.

ALFRED
A most enchanting thought. I must confess, it has been in my mind during
the last twelve hours.

ROSALINDA
My husband will be here any minute.
He must not find you, especially in
that costume.

(*pointing to Eisenstein's gown,
which Alfred is still wearing*)

ALFRED
It's not very good, is it? Ah, but he
should see me as Faust. I am magnificent! What a role, what an aria!

(*starts to sing*)

Salut—
 (*cracks*)
sal—sal—

ROSALINDA
Stop it, stop it!
 (*begins to cry*)
My husband behaved disgustingly—

ALFRED
He certainly did.
 (*crosses to Rosalinda S.R.*)

EISENSTEIN
(*enters from S.L. posing as Blind, wearing Blind's cape, hat, glasses, briefcase
and beard*)

A-ha!!
 (*in Blind's voice, stuttering a little*)

What can I do for you, madame, and
for you, sir?

(*to himself, while music to No. 15
starts*)

Do they look guilty, and will I trap
them!

No. 15. Trio

ROSALINDA, ALFRED
To judge his expression,

EISENSTEIN
I must use aggression,

ROSALINDA, ALFRED
He'll make no concession.

EISENSTEIN
To force a confession

ROSALINDA
Shall I use discretion?

EISENSTEIN, ALFRED
Shall I use discretion?

ROSALINDA
Or make a confession?

EISENSTEIN, ALFRED
Or force (make) a confession?

ROSALINDA, ALFRED
We can't make demands,
We are in his hands.

EISENSTEIN
They can't make demands,
They are in my hands.
Now please describe the situation,
Precisely, all revealing,
Not even one detail concealing,
And meanwhile I shall take notation.

ROSALINDA
The case is rather curious,
You must employ your wit!

ALFRED
It really makes me furious;
That much I must admit.

EISENSTEIN
Alright, then, f-f-furnish me with good
    pretense
On which to base your whole defense.

ALFRED
Last night I had adventures
Of most peculiar kind.
While with this charming lady
In privacy I dined,
By mistake I was arrested
And here in jail confined.

EISENSTEIN (roughly)
You got what you deserve,
You had an awful nerve.

ALFRED (astonished)
Now what on earth is that you say?
Your task is to defend me.

EISENSTEIN (controlling himself)
Excuse the temper I display,
My subject carries me away.
I never would offend you, no,
My task is to defend you.

ROSALINDA, ALFRED
I find it queer
That you appear
In such a rude and angry mood.
You must be calm at any cost
Or else we both are lost.

EISENSTEIN (to himself)
The fact is clear
That things don't look so very good.
I must be calm at any cost
Or else my case is lost.

ALL THREE
You (I) must be calm
Or else we're (I'm) lost.

ROSALINDA
It all was very harmless,
And nothing bad took place,
But if the tale were rumored
I could not show my face.
My husband would most surely
Blame me for this disgrace.

EISENSTEIN (breaking out)
And he would be correct,
Your conduct was abject.

ROSALINDA (astonished)
Now what on earth is that you say?
Your task is to defend me!

EISENSTEIN (collecting himself)
Excuse the temper I display,
My subject carries me away.
I never would offend you, no,
My task is to defend you.

ROSALINDA, ALFRED
I find it queer
That you appear
In such a rude and angry mood.
You must be calm at any cost
Or else we both are lost.

EISENSTEIN (to himself)
The fact is clear
That things don't look so very good.
I must be calm at any cost
Or else my case is lost.

ALL THREE

You (I) must be calm
Or else we're (I'm) lost!

EISENSTEIN

I beg you to review the case,
Each instant to retrace,
No smallest detail to erase.
Did nothing else take place?

ALFRED

These questions are beside the point!

ROSALINDA

What's that?

EISENSTEIN

Let's talk about your case,
Did nothing else take place?

ROSALINDA

But, sir, what do you think of me?
Your point I really fail to see.

EISENSTEIN

Describe your full impression!
Did nothing else take place?
I need a full confession.

ROSALINDA

How dare you!

ALFRED

How dare you!

ROSALINDA

It almost seems as if you tried
To represent my husband's side,
But now I shall indict him.
The shameless monster was untrue!
And there is nothing I won't do
To pay him back in kind and fight him.
Last night he went to a soirée
And flirted with a whole ballet.
To leave they had to force him!
When he comes home, the horrid brute,
He will receive a nice surprise!
I'll give that monster two black eyes
And then I shall divorce him!

ALL THREE

I'll (she'll) give that monster two black
eyes
And then I shall (she will) divorce him.

ALFRED

Now that all is known to you,
Tell us quickly what to do.
Can you give me some advice,
Cure the sinner of his vice,
Make the husband pay the price?

EISENSTEIN

I've heard enough!

ALFRED

Have you gone mad?

EISENSTEIN

Your time is up!

ROSALINDA

Are you insane?

ROSALINDA, ALFRED

What does this language mean?

EISENSTEIN (*with ominous voice*)

Transgressors, taste my fury!
At last vengeance is mine!
You stand before your jury,
(*taking off his wig and glasses*)
For I am Eisenstein!

ROSALINDA, ALFRED
(*flabbergasted*)

His name is Eisenstein!

EISENSTEIN

Yes, yes—I'm the one, who was mistreated
You're the one who lied and cheated
But at last you see the dawn of Judg-
ment Day!

ROSALINDA, ALFRED, EISENSTEIN

You're the one who lied and cheated,
I'm the one who was mistreated.
Now you try to put the blame on me.

ROSALINDA

Eisenstein must resign!
Eisenstein must pay the fine!

ALFRED, EISENSTEIN

This Eisenstein will not decline.

ROSALINDA

Vengeance now is mine!

ALFRED, EISENSTEIN

Revenge now is mine!

ROSALINDA

Pray, hear me out until the end!

ALFRED

Don't jump at false conclusions, friend!

EISENSTEIN

How dare you stand and call me down,
While you have on my dressing gown!

ALFRED

This is your bathrobe, I admit.

ROSALINDA

Too bad it was so good a fit.

EISENSTEIN

This proof they can't refute,
And they both turn pale and mute.

ALL THREE

Vengeance is mine,
Ve, ve, ve, ve, ve, ve, ve,
Vengeance is mine!

ROSALINDA (*to Eisenstein*)

You dare reproach me? *You* speak of
    infidelity, when I—
(*pulling the watch from her bosom*)
when I know exactly what time it is?
(*dangles the watch in front of his face*)

EISENSTEIN

Good Lord, my watch!

ROSALINDA

(*opening her cape, revealing the ball-
    gown, with Hungarian accent*)
Vould you like to count my hearrt-
    beats, "Marrquis"?

EISENSTEIN

Oh, what a fool I am!

ALFRED

Yes, aren't you?

EISENSTEIN

You keep quiet. It so happens that you
    are wearing *my* dressing-gown!

ALFRED

A nasty-looking one, if I ever saw one.

EISENSTEIN (*furiously*)

Take your hands out of my pockets,
    when you say that. I demand satis-
    faction, you wife stealer!

ALFRED

Satisfaction? And so do I! Be so kind
    as to go up to cell No. 12 and finish
    up your term. You already owe me
    one night.

EISENSTEIN

I should serve a term now? Are you
    crazy? Never in a million years. Why
    should I? I'm not Eisenstein. Who
    can prove that I am?

ALFRED (*beside himself*)

Warden, warden!
            (*Frank appears.*)
We need witnesses who can identify
    him.

ROSALINDA

I can identify him!

EISENSTEIN

A wife can't testify against her husband.

FRANK

I think I can help you.
            (*shouts*)
Frosch!

FROSCH

(*enters from S.R. rear, with a pail and
    a horse brush*)
Did you have to disturb me *now?*

FRANK

Go up and get these two girls in No. 13
    and bring them here.

FROSCH (*stubbornly*)

No!

FRANK

Why not?

FROSCH

I was just going to give them their bath,
    warden.

ADELE

(*enters with Sally through gate, goes
    up to Frank, excitedly*)
Warden! Warden indeed! A prison!
    You told us this was a palace! How
    could you do this to us?

SALLY

What have we done?

FRANK

Ladies, it was all a ghastly mistake. I
    beg you to forgive me. Do you recog-
    nize this gentleman here?

ADELE

Why, of course. This is Mr. von Eisen-
    stein. And this is his wife, my ex-
    mistress.

ROSALINDA

(*angrily, to Adele who is still wearing
    Rosalinda's dress*)
And you take off my dress!

FROSCH

(*crossing toward center rear*)
Need any help?

FRANK (*to Eisenstein*)
Well, my friend?

FROSCH

(*re-enters from S.R. rear, followed by the entire company, Orlofsky, Ivan, guests. All are wearing capes and hats. Servants bring champagne and glasses.*)
What a wonderful prison this is! We even have open house.

ORLOFSKY
Well, Falke, what is this all about? Why did you bring us here?

FALKE
Because I want you to see the end of our little play!

ORLOFSKY (*amused*)
You mean that you're going to end it in jail? That's very funny!
(*He laughs loudly.*)
Ha-ha-ha-ha-ha!

EVERYBODY
Your Highness, you're laughing!
(*Music to No. 16 begins.*)

ORLOFSKY
Ivan! Make a note of *that!*

No. 5. FINALE

ROSALINDA, ADELE, ORLOFSKY, FRANK, ALFRED
O, Eisenstein, you master mind,
Your wife has left you far behind,
The braggart with his master wit
Has fallen in the pit.

EISENSTEIN
Won't you tell me out and out,
What is this story all about?
And what are you driving at?

FALKE
It's the vengeance of the Bat!

ALL
Yes, the vengeance of the Bat!
But the joke you played with such a bang
Turned out to be a boomerang.
This time it was the clever Bat
Who gave you tit for tat!

EISENSTEIN
Do explain it from the start.

FALKE
All the anguish you went through
Was a joke I played on you.

ALL
Was a joke he played on you.

EISENSTEIN
And the prince?

ORLOFSKY
I played my part.

EISENSTEIN
And Adele?

ADELE
With all my heart.

EISENSTEIN (*to Alfred*)
But your dinner?

ALFRED
A mere invention.

EISENSTEIN (*to Rosalinda*)
But my house-robe?

ROSALINDA
Stage convention.

EISENSTEIN
That is wonderful. Oh, bless you!
Oh how glad I am to know!
Come, dear wife, let me caress you!

ALFRED (*softly to Orlofsky*)
It was not exactly so,
Why should we start confusion
And end his fond illusion?

ADELE
Well, and what becomes of me?

FRANK
To this jail you have the key:
As a father would approach you,
For the theatre I shall coach you.

ORLOFSKY
(*taking Adele's arm*)
I'm a patron of the arts:
I will sponsor her debut.
It is Orlofsky's motto,
"*Chacun à son goût.*"

ALL
It is Orlofsky's motto,
"*Chacun à son goût.*"

EISENSTEIN (*speaks*)

Rosalinda, forgive your faithful Gabriel! You see, the champagne alone was to blame!

ROSALINDA

Champagne's delicious bubbles,
  tralalala!
Scattered all our troubles, lalalalala.
It taught me something priceless
That husbands are not viceless,—
A wife must be resourceful

To make a man remorseful.
We toast Champagne,
The essence of the essence,
The King of effervescence.

ALL

A toàst, a toast, a toast,
His Majesty we celebrate,
Celebrate, long and late!
Joyously together
We toast Champagne the Great!

END OF THE OPERETTA